CONTRACT WIFE CONTRACT LIFE

Married to the Game ...
10 Step Guide

Dr. Meda Leacock

For Information Contact:
WondaWoman Publishing, www.wondawomanpublishing.com

Written by Dr. Meda Leacock
Typeset: www.impactstudiosonline.com

ISBN: 978-0-578-51899-2 (paperback)
LCCN: 2019905640

Library of Congress Cataloging-in-Publication Data
is available
Printed in the United States of America
10 9 8 7 6 5 4 3 2 1

Dedication

God

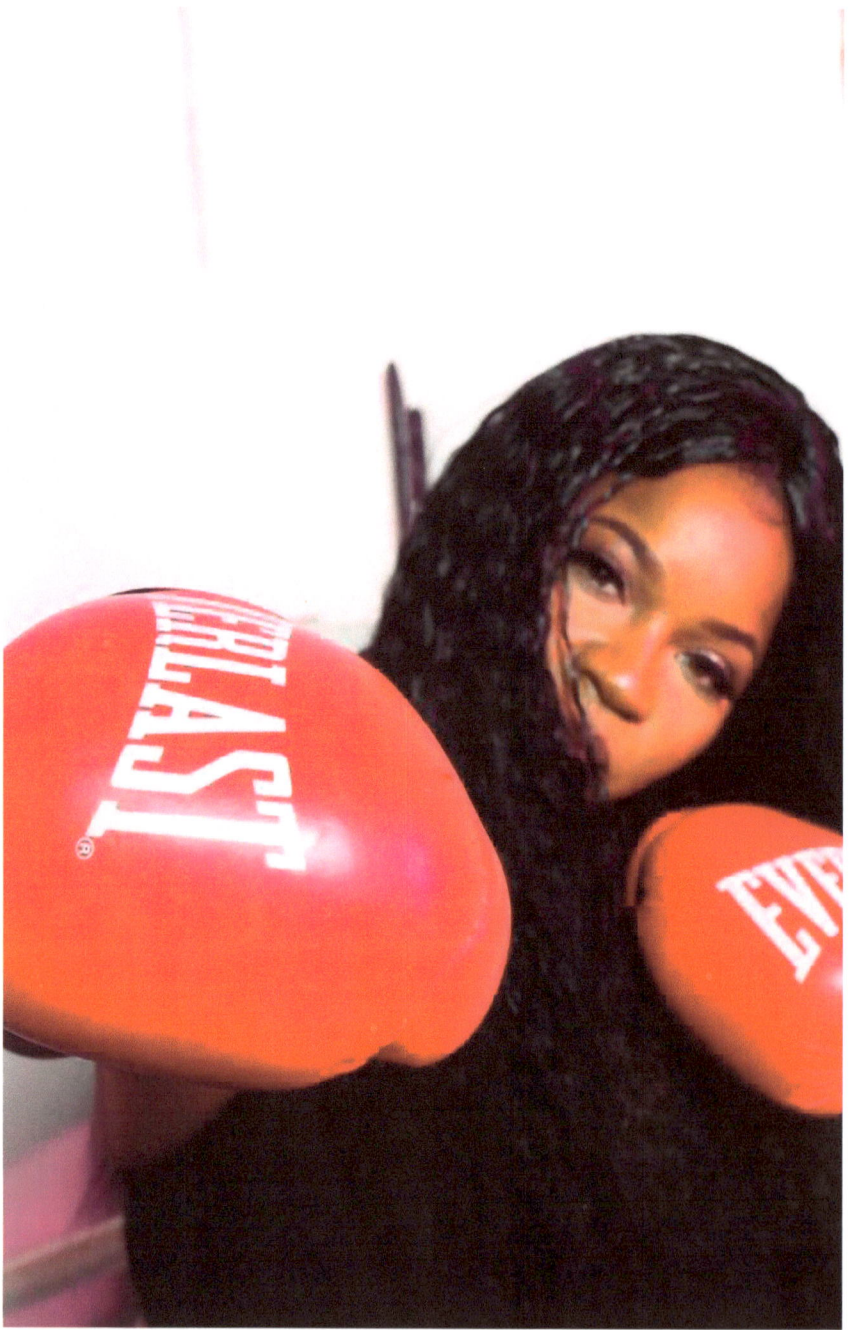

TEAM PLAYERS

I thank God first and foremost, for giving me life, health, strength, patience, & courage. I thank my mom, my backbone & foundation, my dad for instilling fearlessness in me, & my daughter Princess Destiny for the motivation that makes my heart beat. I express my love to my brothers Celio & Pancho, and my lovely sisters Davina, Samantha & Moni, who always have my back. As well, Tia Maura, my goddy Joe, & my entire family.

A special hell yeah goes out to my honorary sisters of God. THE QUEENS... who've been by my side, the ones who have held me down & the ones who inspired me to push forward... Nadia, Charlene, Orphia, Torie, Yulanda, Karen, Chelsea, Kia, Jamila, Tracy, Teri, Jessica, Toya, Richera, Iris, Keenia, Tanya, Aliyah, Stacy, Lati, Xio, Yolanda, Jaquelyn, Sharie, Ayeshah, Tanisha, Olivia, Shana, Tenisha, Asia, Tamika, Danielle, Juliet, Halimah, Jaja, Eve, Sata, Shola, Free, Queen Bee, LisaRaye, Set Shakur, Lil Mama, Isha, Tatia, my IAmWondaWoman fam, my WondaWoman Productions & Boxer Wives fam, my Brooklyn Tech & Schuyler fam, & my Panamanian fam.

Can't forget THE KINGS... my brothers & homies in my life, whom I watched & studied. Henceforth, why I think the way I do... DeDe, Dwight, TJ, Raheem, DV, Rafer, Devyne, Abram, Edgerrin, Antrel, Kimani, Damien, Frank, Monte, Zab, Eric, Barny, Mook, Memphis, Ty, Rap, Twiz, Aaron, Brandon, Myko, Corte, Collin, Ze, Pooh, Webb, Justice, Mack, Steve Rif, Puff, Busta, Ceelo, Deric, Stevie, Nash, Rio, Jimmy, Maino, Tek, SNS, Bang & Cease. And lastly I'd like to thank _____ (Bae). This could be anyone at any given time. Oh you ain't think I was married to the game, & ain't picked up some game... did you?

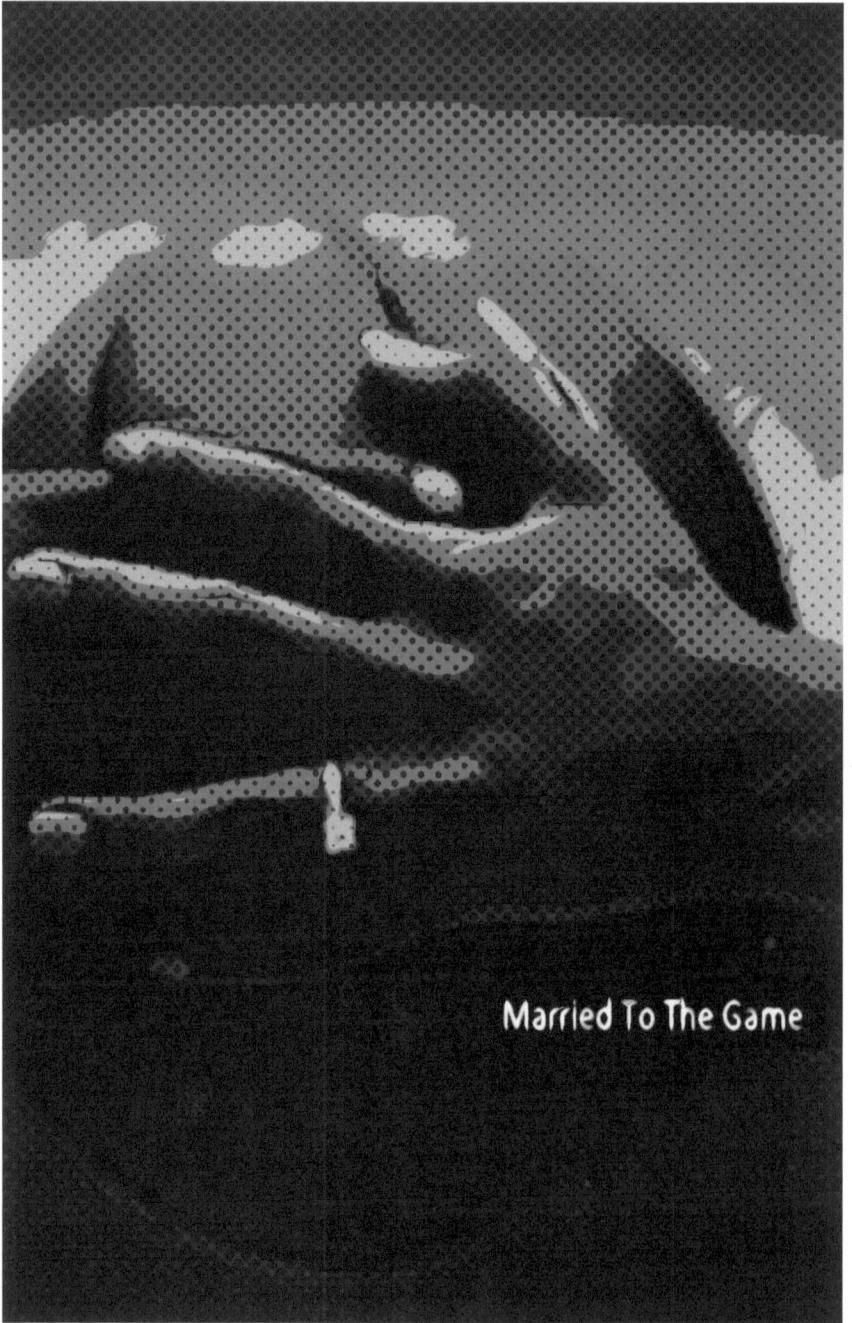

Married To The Game

PROLOGUE

This book is merely based on Experience and a little thing called Opinion.

TABLE OF CONTENTS

Lesson One:
He Sign, You Sign

TEAMWORK MAKE THE DREAM WORK… Once your beau signs a contract, although not physically, you signed right along with him. Every law, rule or trick or trade that comes along with the job is now your responsibility, just as much as it is his. The last thing you want to do is have him and his team believe that you don't completely believe in his quest.

Your life is now aligned to agreements, rules and regulations. As a wife, it's pertinent that you do everything in your power to aid your MAN into following those rules. When he signed his contract, psychologically you signed too. But do remember, if he gets cut from the team; you get cut from the team too. You signed up to be in this together. If the powers that be feel you are not adhering to the plan, they will find it in their kind hearts to see to it that you are no longer important to the plan.

Learn how to be eloquent enough to talk to his employers with intellect and confidence, all while positioning yourself where you need to be to get what your MAN needs. Not too many wives possess the grace and style to manipulate the system respectively. Not too many wives EVEN CARE.

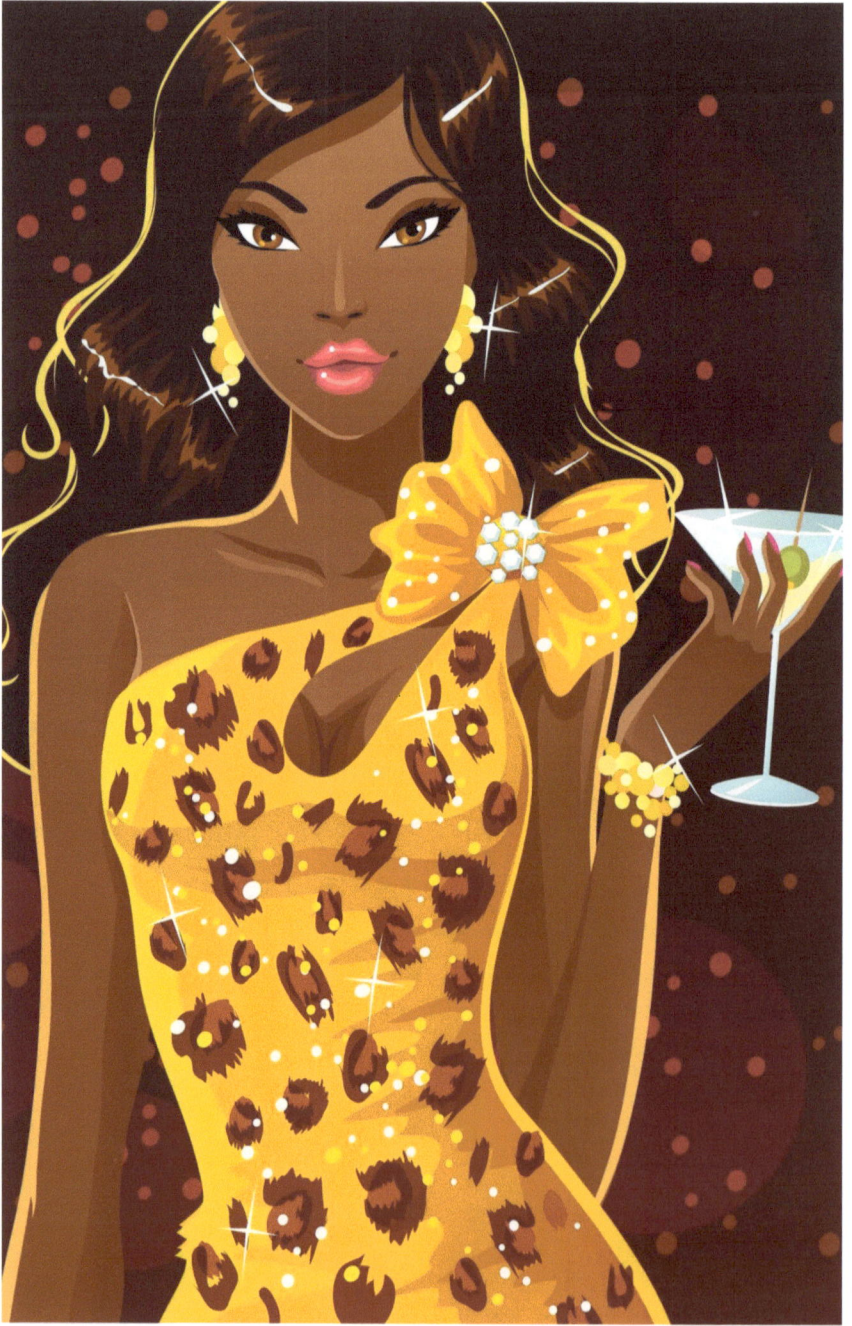

Lesson Two:
Add Value, Become Indispensable

BE A FRANCHISE PLAYER… You definitely don't want to be the Wife that is replaced by the girlfriend who adds value. Most of these athletes have lived a life of various individuals getting things done for them.

The last thing you want to do is come into his life and just exist. You have to pay attention to this man and passively attempt to fill every void that exists. That includes being his wife, his mistress, his momma, his best friend, his spiritual healer, his motivator, and the list goes on.

Although it may look like the wife of an athlete does nothing all day but yoga and shop… on the contrary it takes an immensely strong individual to fill her shoes. She has to be strong yet passive, alert yet oblivious, on top of it yet patient, communicative yet restrained, bold yet reserved, outgoing yet withdrawn, and the list goes on.

Get to know your man, get to know his needs. Be someone he can come to when he has a hard day. Be someone he can come to when he just wants to talk. Be someone he can turn to if he has questions and concerns about life, other than his agent, his lawyer and his business manager. Help him achieve something he always desired that his skill couldn't get him. Give him a different perspective on life and he will continue to come to you to SEEK YOUR INPUT.

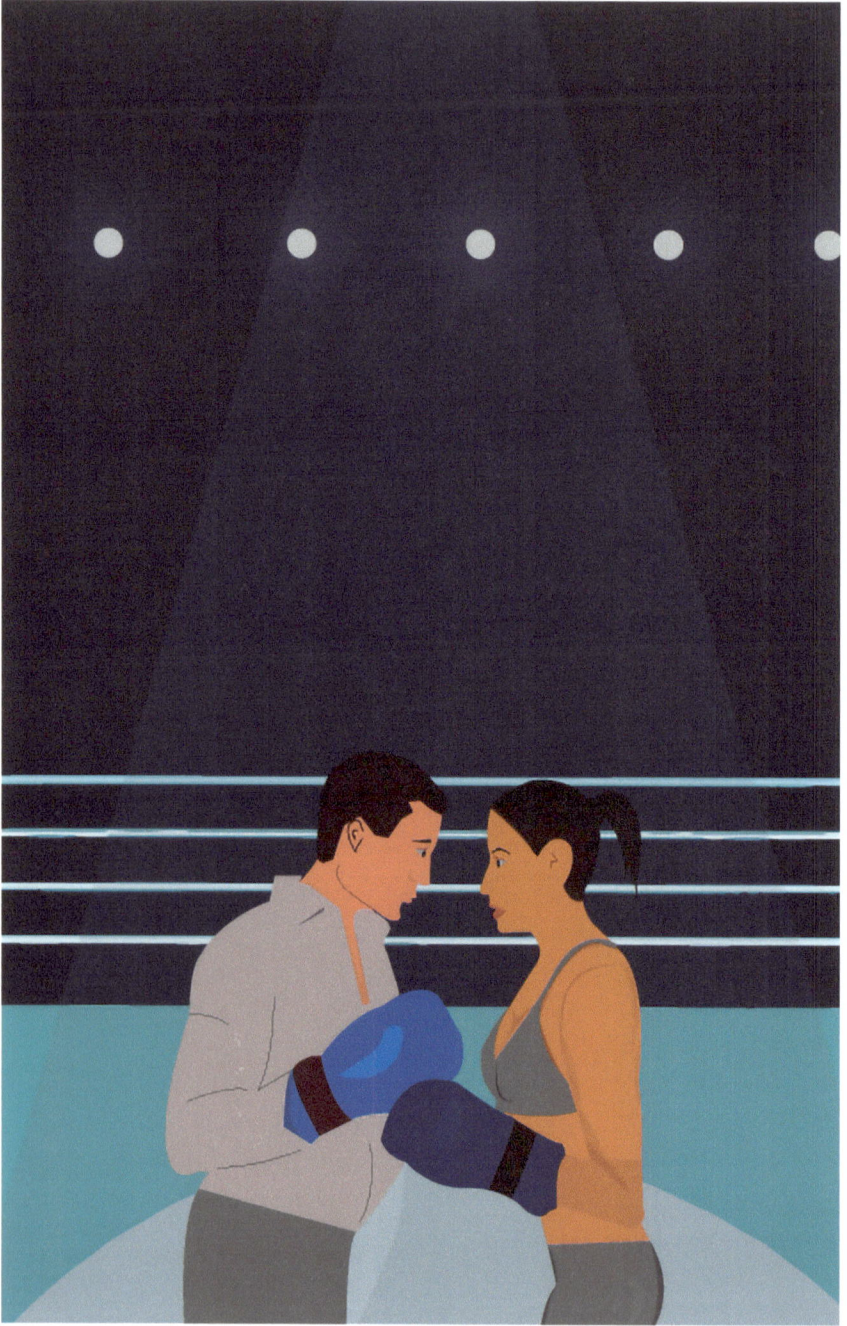

Lesson Three:
Timing Is Everything, Pick Your Battles

KEEP HIS HEAD IN THE GAME… Your livelihood is intertwined with his ability to perform. The last thing you want to do is mentally incapacitate him; it often leads to physical incapacitation. Timing is everything; your questions and concerns for any issues or extra-marital affairs will kindly have to wait until the match, the meet, or the season is over.

I was married to a professional boxer. The rules of fight time entailed no fornication for almost two months, workouts two times a day, irritable weight loss, and training camps for at least a month away from home. I never went away to training camp with him and I never stood in his corner during actual fight time… but minus the actual punches, I felt like I was training for a fight as much as he was. Everyday I would plan my workouts around the same time he worked out. I would never go out to the clubs or hang out with my friends at night during training. I never wanted to break his focus and have him thinking about my whereabouts, rather than his head being strictly in the game. Boxing is a brutal sport, and it was clear to me that any bit of focus lost, could end up costing us everything. I chose to be ALL IN.

Lesson Four:
Put On Your Public Face

GET YOUR GAME FACE ON... No matter what you are going through within the confines of your private walls, the world should never suspect a thing. If you are truly in it for the long hall, the last thing you want to do is allow your family, friends and the public to dictate the faith of your relationship. Any and everyone will chime in, and on any given Sunday, you may not be strong enough not to indulge.

First Lady is human. I'm sure every waking moment of her and her husband's life was not perfect. I'm sure they had various disagreements. However, Mrs. President never went outside without putting on her Public Face. Hey if you just happen to be the exorcist at home, and that works for you guys, you just need to be his saving grace in public.

One thing a lot of people in my family and on the outside told me was that they never had any idea what was going on. I always stepped into those boxing arenas with my head held high. I always stepped into those boxing rings at the end of the fight with the biggest smile on my face. I knew it was pertinent for me to leave my woes at home and show up with nothing but my GAME FACE on.

Lesson Five:
Don't Lose Yourself

STUDY AND MAINTAIN YOUR PLAY BOOK… It is definitely important that you don't lose who you were before you met this man. Do not, I repeat… do not allow your life to wholly revolve around him. Find whatever it is that brings you Zen and happiness and stick to it. You don't want to wake up one morning and not recognize the woman you see looking back at you in the mirror .

Often our close friends are the first to go and the first to not recognize us. Do not leave your best friend behind, as she is often the one that can help keep you as you. Now, you absolutely want to make sure your best friend is someone you can trust around your husband and doesn't resent your new lifestyle as well, but that's a whole other lesson.

If you were in school to get your diploma, finish school. Don't drop out on the account of his success. If you liked working with children before him, perhaps start a charity to continue to work with children. Go take up real estate, coding, accounting, sell hair or clothes, etc. Provide yourself with some sort of vice to REMOVE YOURSELF from the chaos for a few hours a week.

Lesson Six:
Don't Ever Get Comfortable

OPTIMUM PERFORMANCE WINS GAMES… Don't be a boring wife. Keep your relationship interesting. Make your man want to come home because he loves that 'thing you do'. Because you do the things that no one else but you can do.

Heck, an alter ego always worked for me. Pay attention to your man. Become all the women you envisioned he desired. Make up names for each alter ego. Have different looks and personalities for each alter ego. Some days it doesn't hurt to ask your man who he wants to be with, while other days you can just surprise him.

Become his best friend, or better yet his homie. Allow him to express his inner thoughts to you without judgment. Plan fun events and dates you both will enjoy on his days off. Never stop dating your man. While everyman loves comfort from a woman, they also like the feeling of 'new and alive'. This is perhaps a reason that they often stray… the newness, the aliveness, it poses a temporary fix for a void they DEEM TO FILL.

Lesson Seven:
Believe in Hierarchy

YOU ARE THE TEAM CAPTAIN... Know your place in the hierarchy. Of course there are exceptions to everything, but it is my belief that the majority of athletes, especially at the beginning of their careers... CHEAT. There is nothing in life like new money, new egos, and new desires. You are the team captain, however, unless you are going to fight every woman that shows up to play, you unfortunately do not possess the ability to BENCH any of his players.

As a WIFE, I get that he looked you in your eyes, put that ring on your finger, and said I DO before God, the pastor, your family and friends. But, the GAME rules and the Church's rule somehow aren't the same. Somewhere in the GOOD BOOK it references that women who have dealings with married men shall be cursed, so allow their faith to be in God's hands. Your job is to ENDURE and OUTLIVE their flings and mistresses.

Sadly, if you want to remain in the TOP SPOT, you absolutely have to mentally go into the situation not putting too much emphasis on his infidelity. Now while I'm not telling you to promote it, I certainly am stating you have to carefully figure out a method to get past it.

Some of my friends understand where I'm coming from by going through their own experiences, but then there are the few that feel strongly that I am insane and that athletes can co-exist in a non-cheating relationship. Once again, I mentioned there are exceptions to every rule. I personally never met an athlete that didn't cheat at some point in their life. However, I'm overly optimistic and it remains to be seen.

Not just athletes, but do all men cheat? It seems to be one of the most thought about and discussed questions in any given conversation. I am only human, and as a human I am allowed to provide my opinion to whoever will listen. YES, it is my belief that all men cheat, at some point, if not throughout their entire life. Although most women grow up reading and watching fairy tales, waiting for Prince Charming to arrive. As crazy as it may sound, I've often had to ask myself should we as women hold cheating so dear to our hearts? Or should we build our hearts up and not leave it wide open for heartache, Pain and continuous disappointment. NO EXPECTATIONS, NO DISAPPOINTMENTS. Because my overly realistic ass... really do believe that Prince Charming cheated on Cinderella, Snow White and Rapunzel, and probably with each other.

The question I have is should women make it a life and death situation and end the relationship because she was cheated on? Being in a relationship is about living with what you can deal with. Being in a relationship with most athletes, or any successful man, is actually living with everything you never thought you were strong enough to deal with.

Now I'm not saying I give my man permission to cheat, like I say "here is a condom, go make sure you give it to her good". No not at all. All I'm saying is if he is going to do it, I would appreciate if he wasn't sloppy and kept his extra marital affairs away from me. I would appreciate it if he made sure his flings knew their place... their level in his food chain.

If a chick ever felt she wanted to step out her place in line and call my phone or make it known to me she is messing with my King, as Queen I need to be able to scream "OFF WITH HER HEAD". She should never have the privilege of meeting his parents, or his siblings, or hanging out with his homies. She should never feel she is anywhere in the vicinity of the level of his Queen.

Lesson Eight:
Lifestyle Over Perfection

HOW MUCH IS THE TROPHY WORTH TO YOU... Do you want a perfect man or a perfect life? You have to choose. I'm not saying you can't have both, I'm just saying I've never met anyone who had both.

For years your parents read you books that had you believing a great big handsome man was going to swoop in on a horse and whisk you away to a mansion full of maids and butlers. It had you dreaming of your long white wedding gown with a train so long it trailed so far down the aisle. It had you visualizing all of your family and friends standing in awe and watching as you slowly made it to the altar to claim your HAPPY ENDING.

Did you ever stop and think why all of those endings were considered happy endings? Did you ever wonder what those women had to endure to stay happy? Did you ever wonder if those women were even happy? Did you ever wonder if those women ever had a choice, considering the next line was always THE END.

Life has taught me that no human being is truly perfect. However, the lifestyle that comes attached to that un-perfect being, for some at least, is as close to perfection as they will ever be. Own that perfection. Learn to look at the glass as half full, rather than half empty, and you will be more grateful for the blessings you receive rather than the fairy tales that deceive.

Lesson Nine:
You Can't Change Him

NO FOUL, NO PLAY… Unless you know magic or possess some spiritual abilities to make someone do what you want them to do, stop trying to constantly commit the error of forcing him to change.

You truly are special for the strength, endurance and patience you possess to deal with this man. However, you are not that special that he will actually change for more than a moment.

Until you can sink it into you mind, brain and heart that you do not possess the powers to CHANGE ANYONE in the whole wide world… life as an athlete's wife will be so difficult for you.

Most people change when they have life altering experiences such as near-death experiences, someone close to them gets sick or dies, and accidents. Others change temporarily when they are threatened with change or loss. However, the key word we need to pay attention to is temporarily. It often seems that when the universe tilts back on its axis and life becomes familiar or comfortable again, the pre-change individual reappears.

Other instances of change also include plain old MATURITY. And no one I ever knew ever had a clue when the Goddess of Maturity would ever show up.

Lesson Ten:
Makes No Sense To Keep Score

PLAY CHESS NOT CHECKERS... If you are going to sit around and tally up everything that your Man does... then this is definitely not the gig for you. GUILT IS ALWAYS BETTER THAN ANGER. As I stated before, learn your man... assess his level of guilt with your level of rewards.

You ever heard the term "wrong and strong"? Sometimes going to bat with him will only make him angrier. Remain calm and collective. Don't give him the pleasure of knowing your level of anger. Sometimes it scares them tremendously when they don't have a clue what we are thinking. Don't allow him to see how much invisible steam is blowing out your nose. Do allow him to sit and marinate in his guilt, as it almost always works out in your best interest. Men don't change because you want them to. Men don't change because they said sorry. Men only begin to change involuntarily when their internal clock reaches its capacity of damage.

You ever heard the term "if you can't beat them, join them". If you have no desire to leave this man, especially not for infidelity, figure out how to make yourself just as happy as he made himself with his shenanigans, through GUILT AND REWARDS. Play CHESS NOT CHECKERS. Playing checkers entails finding any opening to make your move. Playing chess entails carefully thinking out your moves to gain the most leverage.

OFFENSIVE CHECKLIST

_____ I'm strong yet passive.

_____ I'm alert yet oblivious.

_____ I'm extremely patient, I pick my battles.

_____ I communicate yet I am restrained.

_____ I am bold yet reserved.

_____ I am outgoing yet withdrawn.

_____ I have learned to control my emotions.

_____ I am an asset to my man.

_____ He can't get enough of me in the bedroom.

_____ I am the foundation in my relationship.

DEFENSIVE CHECKLIST

_____ I have no patience.

_____ I am a jealous secret spy with my man.

_____ My communication is horrible.

_____ I have no restrain.

_____ I cannot control my temper or emotions.

_____ My life completely revolves around my man.

_____ I am slightly insecure.

_____ I bring no spice to my man's life.

_____ I stopped or never provided motivation

_____ I hardly communicate with my close friends anymore.

VENT EXERCISES

These pages are for you to vent. It's often better to write it down, than to say it out loud. Everything that runs through your mind shouldn't be said. Often after you have vented and gotten it out of your system, you don't even have the desire to confront the issue in the manner you were going to while you were emotional and heated.

Perhaps you just want to write 'I'm married to the game' over and over to mentally stimulate your brain through repetition. It's sort of like the way our teachers used to make us write a phrase over and over, as they thought we would eventually believe what we were repeatedly writing.

Vent: I'm Married To The Game…

Vent: I'm Married To The Game...

Vent: I'm Married To The Game...

Vent: I'm Married To The Game…

Vent: I'm Married To The Game...

Vent: I'm Married To The Game...

Vent: I'm Married To The Game…

Vent: I'm Married To The Game...

Vent: I'm Married To The Game…

Vent: I'm Married To The Game...

THE END

www.ingramcontent.com/pod-product-compliance
Lightning Source LLC
Chambersburg PA
CBHW041215270326
41930CB00001B/31